Angel's Hell

By Fereshteh Coley

Angel's Hell

ISBN-13: 978-0692389935
ISBN-10: 0692389938

Book & Cover Layout by HER Enterprise
Editing by Shalis Ricks
Front Cover Photo by © Depositphotos.com/ I_g0rZh

Dedication

To all my Domestic Violence survivors and to the ones who are still in the battle; May God cover you and continue to cover you.

To my Parents, it's because of you I had the courage to go on.

To my Son, it's because of you I had the courage to keep on.

To my support system; God place people in your life, some for a season and some for a lifetime, whatever part you played, I thank God for you.

Last but not least, to my Lord and Savior Jesus Christ, because You turned it, I am still here!

Table of Contents

2   Introduction

6   They Don't Know My Story

18   A Visit From Satan Himself

34   Angel's Journal Entries

45   The Little Heartbeat

59   When Will Enough Be Enough?

75   Is Hell About to Be Over?

92   Seeing Death Before Her Eyes

96   Trying to Close This Chapter of Hell

99   The Mental Hell

107   Happy Days Trying to Uncover

109   Forgiveness

INTRODUCTION

Hell, everybody's hell is a different one. The feeling of being trapped or extremely overwhelmed with thoughts or even life can make one feel like they are living in hell; when your life is out of order or you feel there is no way out of your situation, even if there is a way out, you may feel that you just don't know how to deal, that's what some may feel as their own hell. Me personally, I have dealt with some mental issues and torment that most people could not imagine. The mind has a way of simply playing tricks on you. The mind can allow you to make up scenarios in your head and cause you to react to those thoughts. I have asked myself this question, "How do I make the mind games stop?" As I sit here and think about my journey of writing this book, I can't help but to be filled with mixed emotions. I think about how I will be exposing my wounds and insecurities as I share my story, but I will also be able to use my story to help other women in similar situations to be healed, to be delivered, to be set free and to be able to have the abundant life God intends for us to have.

As a woman, I know other women may have thought to themselves, why we experience so much pain and why as women do we give so much of ourselves even when it seems that we get so little in return. There were many days in my life when I just remembered feeling numb, wanting to feel numb, or wanting to have a hardened heart in order to protect me from further hurt, heartbreak, rejection and pain. I can remember saying that "I will not love and I will not hurt again" or "I wouldn't give my heart to another man, friend, or church." I can also remember saying those famous words of a woman that has been broken or damaged, "I'm done!" As I look back over some journal entries, which I will be sharing throughout the book, I can clearly see and still feel the hurt and pain of a young girl who was suffering from many things. I can hear the cry out and the scream from within her soul. As you embark on this journey with me, you will be able to observe the repeated questions and self-doubt. Looking back, I can see how the devil had a trap set to destroy me. I can see his strategic plan to kill me and stop me from my God given destiny.

This battle is not a battle for just the unsaved. Even after accepting my calling and gift and living for Christ, the enemy had a way of playing on my desires which often led me to lose focus and end up on the same road of pain. I must warn you, this book is real. I am allowing myself to be transparent and I am finally opening up and talking about my real struggles so other women who are going through these same experiences can be delivered. I thank God for deliverance, I thank God for healing, but He could not begin to do those things until I exposed the enemy and expose my pain and deep hurts. I knew that in order for me to heal, I had to be willing to expose my wounds. Now I am set free and know the real meaning of grace and mercy and forgiveness from our Father in heaven. The torment I experienced was real, the fear was real, the hurt was real, the disappointment was real, the depression was real, the desperation was real, the agony was real, the cries was real, the beatings was real, and the journal entries you will see are real.

I share my pain so you can see that you are not alone and there is a purpose behind the suffering. God can use our pain to get our attention and point us to our destiny. I am learning that some things I allowed myself to experience God had literally turned it around for the good. Certainly pain does not feel good but helping another does. I have learned the true meaning of working out for my good and His glory.

THEY DON'T KNOW MY STORY

The enemy can throw some pretty hard blows and knock us down if we're not prepared or grounded in God's word. Well honestly, you can think you are prepared and he can still hit you with something that will knock you off balance. Just like a ship torn by the raging sea, we can get torn into many pieces mentally, emotionally and spiritually and that can also take effect on our physical being, meaning you can become ill behind the things you are going through; and that's what was happening to me. I was a lot of broken pieces trying to mend myself back together. Until one day, the Lord got a hold of my emotions and let me know, "Daughter you can make it on broken pieces." Circumstances may seem broken in our lives but we can make it if we just hold on to His hands. Just read it in the Bible in Acts 27:44 KJV, when Paul survived the ship wreck "And the rest, some on boards, and some on *broken pieces* of the ship. And so it came to pass, that they escaped all safe to land." Not only do we make it on those broken pieces, but we survive and keep living. I know we often wonder why did the storm come or won't go away when we want it to or why so much pain, why so much rejection, why so much hurt, why the lack of, just why me Lord; and how can I heal, Lord knows I want to heal, I want to love, I want to trust again, I want peace, I want to do Your Will, I want to live the abundant life You promised. When we fail to walk by faith or see the manifestation of His promise we start to think, "Well maybe just maybe He does not hear me and I am supposed to suffer forever, maybe because I sinned so much now this is my punishment." If that's the conversation you begin to have with yourself, Stop it, the devil is a liar, you can heal and you will heal. Jesus defeated death, hurt, pain, rejection, insecurities, depression, confusion, lack of and hell at the cross. Serve Him and wait on Him, for Isaiah 40:31 KJV says "But they that wait upon the LORD shall renew [their] strength; they shall mount up with wings as eagles; they shall run, and not be weary; [and] they shall walk, and not faint."

I use to ponder over those thoughts a lot when it came to the situations in my life and even children. Yes, I said children, the children who have been molested and abused, I often wondered why them, they're so innocent and can't defend themselves. I still don't have the answer but I do believe why it touches my heart deeply. Depending on how young they are or even the environment they grew up in or is growing up in, how do they know what to do, how do they wait on the Lord, how do they know that Jesus will protect them if they are not being protected. I would often feel sorry for children that are born in this world, not for the lack of love for them although that is always a concern but because of the evil in this world. There are children of all ages that's being physically, verbally and/or sexually abused and that hurt's my heart because of their innocence. The people that prey on these innocent individuals are sick and we as people of God have to keep praying and fasting as well as take action, especially for our families. This kind of evil does happen in our families and people are often quiet about it. This affects me this way because I experienced it firsthand. This is something that has stayed with me throughout my life although I was keeping it hidden. Once I released and exposed it, the healing began.

When I was about seven years old, I remember family members coming to visit from the South. I was young and excited that I had someone else to bother other than my baby brother and parents. Well after enjoying the family it was of course bed time. Due to the lack of space, we all had to double up in the beds; well nothing is wrong with that because we were family, right? Wrong... I decided to double up with my older cousin who I looked at as a fun person to play with so that was my favorite (he at that time made me feel spoiled). We had all fallen to sleep and the next morning, I remember waking up to his hands in my underwear. This "cousin" who was a young boy (around 12 or 13) now appeared to me as a scary monster that was playing with my privates while I was sleeping at night. At that time I did not know how to quote a scripture, I did not know how to pray, I did not know how to put on a prayer cloth and speak in tongues. I remember at that time feeling darkness and heat in the room. I remember not being able to breathe and I began to sweat but remained frozen. I had no idea what to do. I did not want to cry because that would have told him I was awake and aware of what he was doing and for some reason I did not want him to know that. I knew this was wrong but I

9

was terrified. The only thing I knew to do was to move a little to make him stop. Well he kept going so I moved a little harder and yawned then he moved his hand out of my underwear. He got out of the bed and I remained there for hours, frozen and fake sleeping and scared as if the big bad monster was in my house because to me, he was. After lying in the bed that day I can say that as of now which is about 25 years later, I have no memory of how that day went or even the exact identity of who it was other that his description. What I find rather odd is that when asking my mom who was the cousin who visited us she said no child or teenager came with the family at the time. Mmmm that's not right. I remember a teenager's male hand in my underwear. Now I know the enemy plays mind games but I know that the incident was not imagined and it did happened. The family member she recalls is not the one who touched me and was in the bed with me, that member is a lot older and the perpetrator I'm speaking of was not that much older than myself. I clearly remember what side of the family he was on but not his name; I'm not that close to that side of the family. I remember that incident clearly; I awake from my sleep and opened my eyes, it was a beautiful sunlight shining through the window, I was very still because I felt a dark shadow come over me and now I realize that shadow was fear. But fear from what? Although I knew what my family member was doing was wrong, I never said anything, I felt so ashamed even at that young age. So when people say that a child is too young to know what they are feeling, that's so far from the truth. At age seven I felt ashamed when I saw certain people from that side of the family, the shame would come back and I wanted to hang my head and hide in a closet away from people. Although I did not experience sexual abuse continually, it still left an effect on me. I would worry for my child, for other children, I would cry and cry and cry all because of the tormenting thoughts of what could be happening or what would have happened. See the war in our mind can leave us as unhappy Christians. The devil plants seeds and if we don't get to the root of it, it grows.

Well that demon did not stay but it did visit again in another person whom I looked to as an uncle when I was about 15 years of age. For his protection and privacy I will call him Uncle Pete. I cannot get into the full details about the incident to avoid conflict, but I will say this happened while waiting for other family and friends to arrive because an unfortunate situation happened. I went off to another part of the house to be alone and he came and sat beside me. He started talking about the situation and as he was talking he put his big nasty hands on my thigh, he grabbed my thigh tight. Now I'm older with a bigger mouth, so you would think I shouted "uh no, what are you doing?" But I did not, instead that shame and fear came back and paralyzed me. I timidly said, "What are you doing?" he said "nothing" and looked dumb. He was getting ready to say something but a friend of the family came to where we were. Although this event was not as bad but I knew it could have been worst. I couldn't help but feel dirty and shameful. The reason being and listen clearly; as adults or even mature "Christians", you are to be aware of what words you are planting into our youth. Back then, my mom and dad was not abusing me verbally but there were other "Christian" adults that were planting seeds of negativity in me. Saying and being involved in conversations that were either not true, or if it was, it was time for them to pray for me, not gossip or make it worse. So because of that incident along with the horrible things that was said about me, I would often feel nasty, ugly, ashamed, and low about myself. As Christian adults that have charge over the youth, we are to be examples and should diffuse gossip and not participate in it. Gossip can damage people, it damaged me. The lies and gossip coming from adult "Christians" hurt and damaged me. At that time, it made sick and tired of "church people" and I promised, the moment I am old enough to not be around them I wouldn't. The Bible says in Psalms 34:13 NKJV "Keep your tongue from evil, And your lips from speaking deceit." Our youth face a lot; don't make it worse by adding to their insecurities with evil and lies. Uncle Pete apologized later for what he attempted to do, but I never seen him the same and definitely would not come around him anymore. The enemy was out to destroy me but God did make a way of escape. The enemy knew I had a purpose before I even knew it but even in that trauma the Lord was right there. Looking back over my life help me clearly to understand the Word of God where it says, "I will never leave you nor forsake you," written in Hebrews 13:5 NKJV.

Other than those incidents, my child hood was pretty much sheltered. My parents tried their best to keep me and brother protected and safe from the outside world. They tried; I can say the enemy does find other ways to try to destroy and think he discredit you. For some reason, I have wanted to be accepted and I would look for love in guys. It was not like my parents didn't love me or I was continually abused sexually, but I see that the onetime I was sexually abuse as a child had future affects. I wanted a man or boy to want me and love me and make me feel safe, I wanted those things but really did not know how that felt or what it looked like.

Looking for acceptance and love, I would find myself in situations that I should not have been in, for example, going to the hotel with a guy that I did not really know. Don't get me wrong, no means no, but I knew better to go and had a feeling in my stomach when he pulled up at the hotel. This incident occurred right at the end of my senior year in high school. An older lady introduced me to this guy that she worked with on her full time job. We talked, we went out and we had a good time. One night he called me and spontaneously wanted to go out, so we did. Then after dinner, he drove around and next thing I know we are parked in front of a hotel.

He stated we should get a room so we can continue talking and I went along with the idea; now don't get me wrong, I had that feeling in my stomach that said stop, not a good idea. I also talked myself out of it by saying that he knew my friend and nothing would happen. Almost as soon as we got in the room, the guy started being very provocative and saying things, he started coming towards me and I started backing away. It was a chase for about 10 seconds then he firmly laid me on the bed. I said no, one time, and then I couldn't breathe. The guy being who he was did not care of my feelings and continued to lay on me and finish his business through my tears and the squirming. I didn't tell anyone at the time but the lady who introduced us. She decided to call the guy and argue, but that back fired on me, because of course he called me every name he could think of and a liar being one of them. Not long after that the countless suicide thoughts followed.

Don't get the idea that this is a tell-all book but rather a book that shows that I'm still alive. I made it and so can that hurting person who feels there's no way out. How did I make it? The hand of God and the Word of God; when I wanted to give up on myself God would send an angel or a word. No matter where I was, God met me there and let me know that He is the Sovereign God.

Not only did I have suicide thoughts but also very bad nightmares; some of which where I felt demonic spirits upon me. I have heard some people say it's the witch riding your back, but what I was experiencing was not that. I was wrestling with this thing while it tried to cover my mouth so the name Jesus would not come out. The first time I had this experience was when I was about 15 years old and I was living with my dad in Washington DC. My stepsister and I at the time were sleeping on the couch because we fell asleep watching a movie and we decide to bunk in the living room. As I was sleeping I felt something with weight begin to lie on my stomach, but it was not like a human or something I could touch, but it felt like a dark spirit and before I could say anything the weight of it was on me. Then, I remembered trying to get up and move my body but nothing would move, so I tried to scream and felt like something was over my mouth, like a muzzle or something; so the living room table was in kicking distance, I struggle to kick the table and I finally was able to kick it over but no one awoke. So somehow I

16

was able to utter "Jesus, Jesus, Jesus" until that thing went away. When it finally left after saying Jesus, I was able to raise up and look around, my brother was still sound asleep, my step sister was still sound asleep and the table had not been touched. I was so out of breath as if I had been in a physical fight, but I see with my spiritual eyes now, just like the Word of God says in 2 Corinthians 10:3-4 KJV, "For though we walk in the flesh, we do not war according to the flesh. For the weapons of our warfare are not carnal but mighty in God for pulling down strongholds," Although I remember being so terrified that I could not go back to sleep; at that time I did not understand what was going on. Now I know that the enemy was trying to destroy me. He knew who I was created for and the enemy does not care about age, he just wants your soul. He does that by trying to steal your joy because he knows the joy of the Lord is your strength. The enemy does not want you to hope or have faith. He wants you to give up. Don't give up on God, seek healing, seek help, and seek Jesus.

A VISIT FROM SATAN HIMSELF

At age 20, I decided to do the strip club thing for about a month, if that. I got no satisfaction there, just embarrassment from exposing my insecurities (meaning the action). I would look for attention with those guys because I was hurting, and I had some issues that could not be explained. Taking off my clothes was an act of exposing myself which also exposed my insecurities of not being loved. I also found myself still feeling uncomfortable stripping, to the point that I was never fully naked; I always made sure that I was in a bathing suit or lingerie of some sort. The devil had my mind to the point that I was crying out for love from a man, any man. In that short period of time, I met up with a couple of girls that I befriended who was also in the industry. These young ladies decided to introduce me to their "brother", in which they called him. I later found out this guy had been locked up for pimping and instead of having prostitutes he would pimp women by putting women in strip clubs. This man was still taking their money and controlling them. This guy just couldn't stand to be around me. He never looked me in my eyes or even held a full conversation with me. I remember feeling hurt because this guy would not even acknowledge me and I didn't know why. I was so consumed in my insecurities that it never came to me that I was seeking attention and acceptance from a pimp. Well I never got the acceptance from him, I didn't understand why until later in life. Later in life when I realized and believe what 1 Peter 2:9 KJV says about me, "But you are a chosen generation, a royal priesthood, a holy nation, a peculiar people." Even then the Lord had His mark on me. I was singled out even then.

I stripped only to come up with enough money to move out and have three months of rent in hopes to have who I thought I was in love with come back home. That's right; I did that for a man. This chapter of my life was when I met my son's father. When we met it was nice at the time. We met at a club that I had been recruiting models at. He had given me his number at least three times and I still had not called him. He came to club time after time just to dance and talk to me. In the beginning, the getting to know each other stage, he was sweet, nice and respectful. We would dance in that club all night and all he would do is kiss me on the cheek. The very last time in the club, he said he was not giving me his number any more but he was going to take mines. I gave it to him and he called as soon as we left the club to make sure it was the right number. We had some laughs and some good times for a while until the devil took off his mask.

Between the ages of 19 and 24, I was in a relationship with my son's father. Soon after giving him my number, the drama really begun, but I was so blinded by issues that I just sat there and put up with it. The first time he slapped me was when I went into DC to pick him up because his car broke down and he was drunk. I can't even remember the reason for the slap but I remember him slapping me, him getting out the car and me running after him. Needless to say, I stayed with him. We moved in together and the saga continued. I would come home to females sitting on the porch. I would go in the house and see that all of my clothing was covered, to appear as if no woman lived in our apartment at all. I remember a time where he fought my little brother like he was a grown man in the streets. My brother is tall so people tend to get intimidated by his height, but still no excuse to putting his hands on a minor. He had his way in scaring people close to me. He shot a BB gun at one of my closest friends at the time for no reason at all, he also scared another friend of mine to the point that she would not want to come around me anymore, as a matter of fact he did that to two of my closest female friends. I believe that was his way of trying to take away my support system. I would find bras in his car and a lot a feminine and sexual products or underwear lying around in his car. Somehow he convinced me that he was not cheating. Actually he did not convince me but I would want to believe him knowing he was a liar.

By now the abuse had gotten worse and I allowed it. His mom knew about the abuse and just made up excuses for him. She would ask me what did I do, or say things like he needs a job or he's just stressed out. The famous "battered woman" phrase. She would try her best to convince me that that it was normal behavior. She would actually say that my situation is not that bad. Well I knew enough to know that it's not normal behavior and it's not right, I was just so ashamed by it and didn't know what to do to get out of it. Mainly because I did not want to be alone and I wanted to betray that I was finally fulfilled and happy and that was so far from the truth. I was so empty but yet full of pain. At this time anything would trigger the punches. Not answering him correctly, giving attitude because he cheated, not answering the phone when he called, anything he did not like would trigger a punch or a slap. I remember when he broke his toe; he had to be rushed to the hospital. I don't know how he got there but I know he called me to come pick him up from the hospital. Well when I got there he was there waiting with his male cousin that was staying with us, his cousin's girlfriend and his cousin's girlfriend's friend which was of course a female (yeah picture my face). I suspected something between the two of them but I kept quiet because if I would have said something he would have hit me in front of everybody. You know, when I think back, he treated his prostitutes better than he treated me; imagine what that did to my self-esteem.

When they got in the car I didn't speak. I was angry and trying to avoid confrontation with him but I look at her as to say, "I'm going whip that butt!" As we were driving, he stated he wanted to make a stop and I said ok but hurry because I'm going to go see my mom; I would often visit my mom when I wanted to get away or feel some love. So he then yelled, "What, you going to leave me and I have a broken toe?" I replied, "Yeah, you're ok, you have Chris." He then proceeded to call me names and push my head in front of them while I was driving. I can remember thinking I can't believe he is doing this in front of that female that he's probably sleeping with and she is probably looking at me and laughing. I remember thinking to myself, that this cannot be love and why does he disrespect me in front of people and why would that girl want this man who is not even treating me like a woman but a dog. Oh the wars of the mind.

A couple of months later, I then found out he was sleeping with that girl. I knew it but had no real proof. Well Chris, Derrick's cousin, was cheating on the female's cousin and she wanted information from me. So I called her phone and played the friend role trying to get information from her. I told her what I knew and vice versa. I was hurt and at that time I wanted women like them to feel my pain. So she told me things, I told her things, but when I confronted him about it, he of course

23

lied and asks where I got my information. I told him that Chris' girl called me. So they called her and she told them what happened and how I called her. He didn't beat me for that, but he did beat me the next day for something else, lying. I told Derrick that I was going to the car to get a CD book but decided to go to the store just to get away. When I got back, he was livid. He began to yell at me and started kicking, slapping, cursing me out and making me feel worthless. So I left when he went to sleep, he called the phone and begged me to come back home and said just don't lie to him again. I believed him. When I got home, the girl he was sleeping with was there, I proceed to jump on her but he grabbed me and took me to the room. Mad, I told him I was going to the store and that I'll be back, but in reality I was going to see my mom. I needed to feel love, well it took me a long time to get home and when I walked in the door he asked, "What took you so long?" I told him "I stopped past my mom's house." After the word "house" had left my mouth, I felt a slap across my face. Derrick beat me again that night and said it was because I kept lying.

About three months later, we moved into our second apartment together and the secrets of a man who convinces women to have sex or perform sexual activities for money, to exploit their bodies and feel good about it overflowed. These women actually thought this was the way of life. They were defiling each part of their bodies and did not care about the consequences. They thought that prostitution was the right thing to do. Then I thought all types of evil and judgmental thoughts about them, mainly because they played a part of my hurt. They were monsters in this movie called Angel's Hell. I did not realize then what I know now, that they too have a hurt or issues that needed to be healed and them acting out that way is a cry out for help. This was the man I was living with, the man that I was in love with and the man that I was scared to death of. So often I would leave and run to my mom's house time after time and he would chase me and drag me, (literally) back to the apartment. If I didn't run to her house, I would hide somewhere and sleep in my car. Of course each time it was a "welcome home" party with his fist. Why I didn't stay gone, why I did not tell; FEAR, fear of being alone, of drama, of death, just me wanting so bad the love in return that I gave out to him.

I remember before I got pregnant I had decided to get a new cell phone number. So this day, he was mad for whatever reason, at this point who knows. I was about to leave my mom's house and he once again decided to pick me up. He followed me home in his car and I was driving mine. When we stopped at the red light, he jumped out his car, grabbed my cell phone and went back into his car. When we pulled up to the apartment, my windows were rolled halfway down. He parked his car, ran up to my car, punched his fist through the window and started to strike me in my face. He then opened the car door and dragged me out while continuing to fight me. Derrick then dragged me up the stairs into the apartment. Once in the apartment, he continued to yell and hit me. I still had no idea what was wrong and what triggered this war. Once we were in the apartment, I saw his mom there so I ran behind her and all she kept saying was, "Stop Derrick" but he wouldn't listen. He then snatched me and pulled me into the bedroom and locked the door. After Derrick locked the door, I looked at him and it was like I saw Satan.

He threw me on the floor and beat me in my face repeatedly. I could see my blood flying everywhere but it did not stop him from beating me. Derrick had me pinned down with my arms down to my side locked between his knees. He continued to punch me in my face for what seemed like hours. Finally, he stood me up and I could remember that he hit me with one last hard punch that knocked me off my feet and threw me into the wall. I could only remember falling and then being unconsciousness. When I awoke, I was in my bathroom tub. I could NOT believe I was in my bathroom tub when I needed to be in the hospital. As I begun to get out of the tub, his mom tried to persuade me to stay there for a moment. She told me that it would not be a good idea to look at my face. So I sat there and begun to touch my face because I could feel that something was wrong and deformed. As I felt through each part of my face, I begun to feel big knots in places that I didn't know could develop knots. I had knots that formed on my forehead, my jaws, my cheeks, and even under my eyes. I could not believe what I was feeling and decided I had to see what I looked like.

I turned to Derrick's mom who had been there through this whole horrific beating and screamed with what energy and voice I had left from my stomach "Leave me alone and get out!" When she departed, I got up to see my face. When I looked in the mirror I couldn't believe the person looking back at me, she was not me. The person I was looking at was something that looked like it came out of a nightmare. My face was swollen; my eyes were blood shot red with dark red veins going through them. Around each of my eyes were rings of black and blue. My nose was swollen and black and blue knots appeared everywhere. The knots were hard and painful. My lips were busted and swollen. After seeing my face, I began to cry and cry, not a loud cry but a silent cry because I couldn't scream and to even talk was painful. All I wanted to do was lay down. As I grabbed my towel, someone knocked on the door and it was no other than the devil himself. When I opened the door, I walked past him but he grabbed my arm and forced me to look in the mirror. He said to me as we looked in the mirror, "Dang man I messed your face up, that means you almost died!" He continued, "I won't do that to you anymore, you look scary," (and I am putting the words nicely, he was much more vulgar in language and harsh), as he made the statements, he made little aww noises as if I was a baby with a minor scratch. As I was leaving the bathroom, I noticed he had company and I did not want them to see what he had done to my face so I ran into our bedroom.

I felt so ashamed and embarrassed. How could he do this to me in front of his mother? How could a room full of guys and his mother allow this to happen and no one be able to stop him? As, I walked into our bedroom, my mouth dropped in disbelief. It looked like a crime scene with my blood. There was so much blood everywhere, all over the walls and the floor. As I stared at the blood covered room, Derrick nicely walked past me and continued to wipe down the blood. I remember feeling faint and I just wanted to lie down. I was so weak that I believe I laid in bed for days. That event caused me to miss about two weeks of work and I made sure that I stayed away from my mom for about two months until my face was completely healed from all scars that I could not explain, well lie about. When I returned to work I remember the embarrassment of people pointing and whispering. My co-workers and other people would stare and when I walk past, I would hear them say, "Dang" or make some type of comment. If they only knew; I already

29

felt shamed and embarrassed, stupid, hurt and the list goes on but the comments just added to the hurt, the embarrassment, the loneliness. This taught me a lesson early on that now when I see hurt people I don't judge them because first, I have no right to, and second, you don't know their story or what hell they are going through. By the end of the first day back at work, the president of the company was there and he called me in his office. I just knew at that moment that I was going to be fired but to my surprise, he gave me a raise. I cannot remember how much but I do know it was pretty substantial. He said to me, "I don't know what happen or who did this to you but I'm giving you this so you can get away from whoever done that to you." I couldn't do anything but begin to cry. Truth was, I was terrified of the person who had done this to me and I didn't want to be alone and too embarrass to ask for help. I was young, pretty and confident when I met this monster. I was active with activities and popular, how could my life take this spiral going down?

As my life and months continued the abuse unfortunately did not cease, but I then learned to try to pray my way through this and often fell to my knees to

30

pray. I didn't know if Jesus was listening but I did not care, it was worth the try. One day while I was on my knees praying, Derrick came in and out of the blue, I felt a hard slap. I couldn't believe that while I was trying to talk to God, while I was trying to feel His presence he had smacked me. I was shocked and yelled, "What was that for?" Derrick's response was shocking, he replied, "Because I know you praying for me to leave," then he sat on the bed and smirked. Many thoughts began to run through my mind, I remember saying to myself, that I was not even safe from this demon praying. This particular incident made me confirm/ assume that I was alone. I felt alone more than ever. What devil would hit a woman while she is on her knees praying to The Most High God?

Not only was the abuse physical, but verbal and emotional. He would do things to make me feel degraded. I remember a time when I was home alone and I would walk around the apartment naked because no one was home. I enjoyed doing this when I was alone because for once I felt free. One day as he walked through the door, he innocently pretended to greet me with a hug and kiss but out of nowhere he grabbed me and we began to struggle back and forth. He then forced me out the door naked. I was naked knocking on my apartment door and he was laughing. All I could think about was my neighbors seeing me naked. He finally opened the door and I could see that he thought it was so funny. I felt so ashamed and then I felt this hot feeling come over me. After that day, I was so ashamed to even look at any of my neighbors because I did not know if they saw me or not. I knew at that moment that this man was trying to destroy me; he was trying to destroy my soul and spirit.

As the months went on so did the drama. Derrick continued cheating and not coming home some nights. He also decided to have prostitutes come live with us and even continued to disrespect me in front of any and every one. I would often write in my journal to try to explain the horror I was living in. Some pages ended up lost but not all of them. I remember giving his mom a journal to read and needless to say it was never returned to me, my guess is she threw it away to save her son. Each journal explained how I was feeling and what I was going through at the time. I was lost, rejected, hurt, terrified; I was everything but free. I would often think, "Where are you

Jesus." The next couple of pages are entries from my personal journal just to give you a taste of what I was going through and feeling.

Angel's Journal Entries

What Reason is He with Me

Him

Go out anytime

Girls cell phone

Get new numbers

Gives out number

Been to club

Sex with other people?

Her

Stays in house

Got number changed

Do not give out number

Have not been to club since we started dating

Had sex with no other since we've been dating

October 14, 2001

- 2 girls on porch; Derrick in the house

October 15th, 2001
- Used condom in pocket
- Lied about being in house alone
- 2 girls in house
- Bedroom clean
- My stuff hidden
- 2 condoms on TV stand
- Phone is off
- Came home 2:00am
- Left out 2:15am, car was here (claim he was playing with remote car)
- Came back in house at 4:45am
- Made phone calls to girls in front of me

October 14, 2001 2:29pm

Although all the things happen, I still stayed. I tried to leave and let him have the apartment and I was going to stay at my mom's house. He said okay, but as I was leaving he shouted, "Stop playing with me!" and he wouldn't let me leave. He explained that I was his only girl. If I had did the stuff he did, it would have been war. I would have gotten hit on, beaten and the guys would have gotten shot. I actually feel that if I didn't come home they would have had sex with these girls in my house. I cried on and off all night. I stayed by his side through everything. I am not stupid, I know that he's cheating, but he won't let me leave. My heart is still hurting even though he feels everything is fine between us. I can't believe he hid all my stuff. That's how I know he was going to cheat. All I want is for

36

somebody to love me. If he loves me like he say he do, why do he purposely hurt me. I'll do anything for him; I'm with him and him only. Why is it so hard to be with me only? Well I guess I just have to let things flow.

Don't care, don't cry, don't question, don't check voicemail. When he leave, you leave even if I am in a hotel or around the corner. Don't come home sometimes this may lead into fights. Try to hold out on sex. I am sure he get it from someone else or he pretend like he do to make me mad.

October 14, 2001 8:28pm

Well today when he got home I was leaving he said not to. We had sex twice. He slept all day. He said he was going to be in the house all day. LIE! When he was on the phone, he asked someone were they coming out. I left for 5 minutes, came back and the two ugly girls were on the porch. I was purposely yelling and calling them names for them to hear. He won't let me leave! Why? The same line (I love him and just want him to act right and want me just as much as I want him.) If he leaves out I'm leaving. If he hit me, I'm leaving.

November 6, 2001 2:30am

While I sit and cry and try to understand, full of worries. While I sit and think about us being together, you are getting pleasure from _____ to feel better. You say it's insecurity on my heart but it's not, it's you, you think you're so bright. You showed me a thing or two since we've been together, which is I'm stupid. I'm a faithful lady who will do anything for you, but for some reason _____ are better for you. Between the naked pictures, personal pornos, open and closed condom in my house. I can't take in no more. I really don't know what a good day is. I have lost myself and you won't let me find me. Well I see that while I worry _____ is having more fun and no worries. It makes you think. Which way do you want to go?

November 21st 4:20am

I have not written you in a while. Well tonight I have no choice. Came in the house at 3:30am. I left at 1:20am or a little before when I let his friend in the house. Where was he? Not with the guys at 3:30am. I am not stupid, he was out living the single life. I sat in the car for this long time. And the whole time I am in the car, I was thinking about him having sex with someone else. I am tired of being hurt. I love him and give him love too much to be treated like this. I'm tired, but I'm not going in that house while he's there. I can't take it no more. And this is my first and last time sleeping in my car. It hurts bad but I got to do what's best for me. I got to make a doctors appt., I've been bleeding for a while and I think they will do a DCA.

I'm not crazy, I don't cry for nothing. I don't have visions for nothing. I know something is not right. I can feel it. I feel it in the hits, the sex, and the conversations. I told him to leave he said okay but he also ran after me and punched me. I'm tired, 20 years old and worn out. If this is love, I don't want it. I'm scared, I know I can't love again. He can live his fun life with all the girls he want, just leave me alone. When I'm at work, I have visions, I can't trust him. It hurts because I love him so much. It hurts because I know the little liking or love he has for me is gone. I can't sleep, I can't even think straight. Love is not supposed to make you cry. I don't know who hurt him but I'm sure hell is paying for it. I'm tired of the hits, of the low words he say and I feel there's no way out, unless it involves pain. Talking do not work. He don't listen, I'm not crazy, just hurt, I'm not crazy, just hurt, I'm not crazy, just hurt. I put myself on the line for him, moved out for him. Do whatever he says to make him happy. Co-signed for his car. It hurts to love and not be loved back!

December 4th

SCARED

I called Chris girlfriend to let her know that she will be okay because she was crying over him. I hate to see women hurt. She is going to tell them that we talked. I tried to deny us talking for the best of both of us. She is still running her mouth. I didn't mean to lie to Derrick but it was for the best. I finally told him I called her first and he was mad. Long story short he is threatening to hurt me when I get in the house.

December 6th

SCARED II

Well nothing happened when I got home. Last night he just said never lie to him again. Well I was in the house last night December 5th hanging up clothes. His phone rung and he went in his friend room and locked the door to talk. That made me mad. So I told him I was going to the car to get the c.d. book. I left and I went to Giant and 2 different gas stations of course he was mad. He whipped my tail. He was hitting me like a _____. My body is sore. I don't know what to do. I'm scared of him and with love you shouldn't be scared or hurt.

THE LITTLE HEARTBEAT

A year and a half has passed and I was now 20 and pregnant. I remembered feeling sad, anxious and yet happy all at the same time. I was sad because I knew in my heart that my child would not have a natural father and anxious because I wanted to know how my life was going to play out. I was never the type of person who wanted to be around or even play with children. I would hold a baby for no longer than 30 seconds then give them back to their parents. I never thought that I would have a child of my own one day. I was happy because I finally had someone that would love me unconditionally, yes I know Jesus loves me unconditionally but I wanted to feel that from a human being, let's be real, a man. In today's society, it seems that people only love with conditions. I love you... if you..., I will divorce you... if you... Now I'm not saying put up with thoughtless and harmful acts, I am saying we all need to be more careful of the choices we make and who we allow ourselves to continue to fall for.

I remember the day I found out I was pregnant. My mom was in the office with me. She was not upset surprisingly. I was having her first grandbaby, although not married, I was technically an adult and I was already on my own. My dad may have been a bit disappointed only because I was not married and he knew that the father was not going to be a father. Again I was happy to have a little one to love and love me back. Now Derrick, his reaction was a different story; he and his mother were not so happy. He already had I believe three children that were various ages. Derrick told me when we first started dating that he did not have any children. Then he changed that story to I have one, then I have two, then I have three. So I was not surprised when I found out later on in life, after I left him for good, that he in fact has over 15 children. He and his mother lied about almost everything. So when they found out I was pregnant, it was not music to their ears. For the first three months, I was under so much stress because he and his mother were trying to convince me to abort. His mother offered to pay for it, she showed me things on her computer; she even tried to offer money and material things to abort my gift.

So when my answer was still a firm no, Derrick and his mom did what they knew how to do and I didn't know they were doing this, but they were doing voodoo. Yes, these people were trying hard to use voodoo to make me lose my precious gift. People voodoo is real but so is Jesus. Later after my baby was born, I found out that he made another female get an abortion the same time I was pregnant. So he had two women pregnant at the same time and can I tell you this was not his first time doing that. May have been more, right now I only know of her. There were many things he did during my pregnancy that was detrimental to me. I remember one day I was sleep in the bed, all alone in the house and I heard him come in the house laughing with the females. I ignored and kept sleeping. I was fed up even then. I felt him get in the bed and call my name; I often fake sleep to avoid talking to him. I said "what" with my back faced to him, (keep in mind I was about seven month's pregnant, high risk pregnancy at that). When I turned around it was a snake looking me right in my face. This man got a snake and had it in my face; I screamed loudly and hysterically, I am terrified of snakes. I grab my purse and ran out the house and drove to my mommy's house.

I called the police so they would knock on the door to scare him. I told the police a pregnant woman ran out of an apartment screaming, which I did and then I climbed in my mommy's bed. I couldn't help but think of how evil it was for him to put a snake in front of a high risk pregnant woman's face or anyone that is terrified of them. I didn't get stomach pains but I had heart pains. That was so evil to do to someone. The whole time I was pregnant I was already bleeding and hurting. I can't help to think that it was due to stress and fear. The enemy not only tried to destroy me but tried to destroy my baby as well. As I think about it, the enemy tried to destroy my natural seed and my spiritual seed. I wish I could say the story ends there but it does not. So much hurt and pain occurred being in that relationship. I remember while still pregnant with Elijah, a good friend at the time (Elijah's godmother) was choosing a name for him. I told her I want my child to have his own name. So she came up with Elijah, which means "The Lord is my God." She chose to do that because my name means Angel. I was excited and loved the name. When Derrick arrived home, I told him about the name and he went crazy. He kept screaming "No, no, no he is going to be named after me". I turned to him and told him

48

no. After all, he wasn't being a father to our unborn. He didn't once go to one doctor's appointment with me; I had a high risk pregnancy which required me to go to two doctors every other week; my regular OBGYN and an OBGYN that specializes in High Risk Pregnancies. I turned to him again and said "No! You crazy, my son will have his own name." I wanted my child to have his own name, his own identity and not anything that reflected Derrick.

I remember so clearly what happened next, I was sitting on the toilet and he came up to me and slapped me very hard and then walked out the bathroom. I was left there crying with blood in my mouth. I called his mother and she spoke to him and after they talked he came back and said, "Fine, you can name him Elijah but the middle and last name will be mine" (I found out after Elijah was born that the reason why he changed his mind because he already had a son named after him). I was shocked, not only did he slap a pregnant woman but he slapped me for no reason. But I should not have been shocked because as I reflect, I remember him putting his hands on me more times than I could count. Weeks went past and it was time to deliver baby Elijah, my gift from God. My mom had surgery about a week before they decided to induce me but she was right by my side despite her pain and her own emotional battle she was going through. Derrick's mom was there too but the person who should have been by my side was out with other women. When he finally decided to get to the hospital, they were just about to give me an emergency C-section because my heart rate and baby Elijah's heart rate were slowing down dangerously. The doctors said that baby Elijah and I were in stress so they took action. They allowed him to come in the delivery room with me, but I did not want him to, I wanted my mommy, after all she was at every appointment I had but one. As they cut me open, Derrick proceeded to tell me everything that was going on. He described my organs they had to take out in order to get to Elijah and the nurse finally had enough and asked him to stop.

On October 7, 2002 at 10:18pm after 12 hours of painful labor, I gave birth to my gift, my personal angel; and all the hell that I went through was gone for a moment. At that moment, I thought about how I had so many complications and I bled the whole time. The doctor thought that I was going to have a miscarriage eventually.

At one point in my pregnancy, doctors did not understand why my body seemed to reject my child or why my child was trying to come out before he had arms or legs. They had to do a procedure to keep my child inside until he developed enough to be born. Between the stresses of his father, the worries I allowed and the voodoo that was on my head, my baby was in danger. But can I say that through this God's word came to life. "No weapon formed against thee shall prosper" Isaiah 54:17 KJV. The weapons were formed and tried to cause harm to us but He who lives allowed my child to live. Elijah was born a healthy baby boy; a loving boy with a loving heart. The devil is a liar and God prevailed. As I reflect back over my life, I know it was and still is the hand of God that keeps me. I recall the doctors putting Elijah on my chest after I delivered him and his little eyes looked at me. I felt so much joy at that moment. He was relaxed and calm and so was I.

They took Elijah off my chest so they could clean him up but Derrick decided that he wanted to hold him, so the nurse wrapped Elijah and let Derrick hold him. As soon as Derrick held him, baby Elijah bald up his fist and cried. I remember this because I thought he sounded just like a little cat. The doctors took baby Elijah so they could clean him up, tag his foot and moved him to the nursery while I was being stitched up. My mommy said she had followed them to make sure they tagged the right baby and no one would steal him, that's mommy, over protective over all her seeds. As they finished stitching me, we were informed that visiting hours were over. So my mom went home and Derrick left too. I was so upset because he wanted to leave in such a hurry and I just had our baby. I laid in my bed feeling alone and in pain from having my baby. I then remember that I was no longer alone because the Lord did send me an angel. I quickly paged the nurse desk and asked if she could please bring me my baby so I could see him. As the nurse handed me my baby, all I could do was just hold him and express my love to him. Just he, I and the peace of God were in that hospital room.

Baby Elijah and I spent about two days in the hospital. In those two days of just being with each other, we were able to bond closer and closer. Over those two days I had one visitor, my daddy. He came to visit us the day after Elijah was born. I felt like a little girl again as we shared many laughs and talks. Although I was an adult now, I still loved the moments where I can feel like daddy's little girl. As I was getting ready to leave the hospital, I remembered wondering who was coming to get me. I knew my mom had had surgery about a week prior to me having Elijah and she was in pain so I didn't want to bother her but I felt like she was all I had. I didn't want to call my dad because if he came and got me, the truth would have come out that I had a no good man. So I called Cheryl, Derrick's mom and she agreed to pick me up. A few moments later, Cheryl called me back and told me that Derrick was coming to pick us up. I said whatever because I had spoken to him earlier and he told me he was not coming because he was busy. I figured she must have called him and fussed with him or something to make him change his mind, who knows. I just kept thinking I just wanted to get dropped off at my mommy's house so I can have peace and get help with my newborn baby. Derrick finally arrived to the hospital to pick us up; we loaded our belongings up and got in the car. As soon as we pulled out of the hospital, Derrick turned the radio up as loud as it could get. I yelled, "No, it's a newborn in the car!" He rolled his eyes and replied, "It won't hurt him." To avoid an argument, I nicely asked him this one time if he could please turn the music down and just take us to my mom's house so that we could be out of his way. He rushed us to my mom's and baby Elijah and I stayed there for about two weeks. It was so peaceful and nice; my mom and I played with Elijah, my dad stopped by and visited baby Elijah as well and for once, I was doing normal things like going to the store without being question or rolling out of the bed without someone jumping all over me to ask where I was going. For those two weeks I felt and looked normal on the outside, but on the inside I was hurt and going through mind wars, after all I only seen Derrick one-time since I was at my mom's house. Our apartment was only ten minutes away and he didn't even come to see me and the baby but one time.

After two weeks of being at my mom's house, I decided to go home and when I got there, there were people everywhere. His prostitutes wanted to see and hold my baby and I clearly with an attitude rolled my eyes and snapped the word "No". I went in my bedroom and Derrick begun to walk towards me so he could get our son.

I don't know what I said or how I said it, but it made him leave my baby right there. He went into the other room and told the girls to come on and they all left the house. Although I may not have been able to protect myself, I promised myself that I was going to protect my baby. During the next couple of days and weeks, I tried not to let things bother me as much and really tried to stay out of his way because I had a baby boy to take care of and I didn't want him to see or pick up those evil habits. I was playing with Elijah about the second week of being there and for some reason Derrick was upset because we wasn't having sex. I explained to him time after time that I could not have sex with him per doctor's orders. This particular day, he decided that he was tired of asking and tired of waiting. I couldn't understand why because he was having sex with his prostitutes. He came in the room to lay down as Elijah was lying in his vibrating bouncing chair playing with the hanging toys. He asked me to lie down and relax with him, so I did. He then proceeded to kiss and touch on me, it had only been four weeks since giving birth and I still was not able to have intercourse yet, I stopped him but he stopped me. He at that time told me to stop playing and forced his self on top of me. It was so painful and all I could do was cry. I was in pain but it was nothing that I could do at the time but cry. I felt so hopeless. When he was done he decided to slap me for crying. He always would slap me for crying, he said that was his way of making me stop crying but it never worked. Now when I say slap I do not mean a small tap but a forceful slap that left hand prints on my face. I just wiped away my tears and took more of the pain medicine. I just sat there and starred, I was shocked and I felt like my soul was numb. I was numb. This caused me to have an attitude and in turn he remained rude towards me so again, I kept my distance and stayed focused on my baby boy.

Me and baby Elijah's six week checkup came and I was so happy. I went to take Elijah to his six week checkup so he can get his shots. When we got to the Pediatrics office they asked for the insurance and I explained to them that I was not the primary and that the baby's grandmother had the insurance information because about a week before the appointment she had put me and Elijah on her health insurance. So the nurse called Cheryl and she confirmed and had to fax over the proof. While we were there waiting, I begun to fill out the required paperwork the young lady working at the nurses' station came over and said to me, "Ms. Coley the proof is here." I said "Thank you" and as I proceeded to sit down, the young lady said to me with a puzzled look on her face, "Look I'm not supposed to give this to you but I think you should have it", and she gave me the proof of insurance. On the paper and to my surprise, I saw that Cheryl not only had me and Elijah insured but she had, me, Elijah, Derrick, her husband, one of Derrick's child's mother, and two of his other children. That was the day when I found out that the child who he said was not his was the child that was named after him and on the health insurance. I was surprised but at this point numb. I looked at the paper, sat down and thought to myself, "another day in hell, it's always something." My baby got his shots and he was such a good baby, he did not even cry until the third shot. I assume my baby was thinking, "They better stop sticking me." It's a joy, babies are a joy. After finishing with Elijah's checkup, it was time for my checkup. The doctor checked on my cut and said I was healing well. After leaving the doctor's office I decided to get lunch at a restaurant just to be able to eat and enjoy the baby Elijah.

As I headed home, I thought to myself, "This crazy day does not feel over." And it was not over.

WHEN WILL ENOUGH BE ENOUGH

I had that feeling of, "something is getting ready to change or something crazy is getting ready to happen," on the way home. I really wish I could have avoided going home but I knew I had to. I slowly pulled up into the parking lot and I sat there for about ten minutes, then I got the urgency to go inside so I decided to go ahead in and get the feeling over with. I got Elijah out of the car and carried him in his car seat to the door. Our apartment building was a secure building so you had to have a key or you had to be buzzed in to get through the front door. As I walked up the stairs and my heart began beating so fast and nothing had happened yet. As I approached my front door, I starred at it and did not want to put my keys in yet. It was like my spirit left my body and my body was just standing there. I snapped out of my daze and slowly and quietly put the key in the door. I walked in, I held onto Elijah's car seat tight. The TV was on in the living room and so were the lights but no one was in there. So I proceed to walk towards my bedroom and pass the second bedroom and the bathroom on the way. As I walked by, I could see his cousin in the bathroom brushing his hair and one of his prostitutes just sitting on the floor mattress in the second bedroom. She looked at me and I starred at her. She looked towards my bedroom door but she didn't say a word but it was like I read her mind and she was saying, "He sleeps with all of us, see for yourself," so I did. When I opened my bedroom door, there was Derrick with a woman on top of him in my king sized bed. Before he could realize that I was looking she had stroke up and down on him twice.

I put the car seat down by the door and I stated very calmly, "So I can leave now, that's my proof and I can walk away." At that moment for a brief moment, I just knew I was free. I just knew I was going to be able to leave without a fight. "So I can leave now?" I asked with a smile on my face, I picked up the car seat and turned around to walk out and I heard the devil say no and grab my arm. I turned around and it was Derrick. I looked at him and I put the car seat down by the bathroom. I yelled, "No, no are you serious?" He just started joking and laughing like I was crazy. He told me that I was just dreaming and nothing was really happening. I picked up the car seat and headed toward the front door. I started to feel the heat rise from my body and I knew I was becoming extremely angry. I decided to put the car seat by the front door and I went back towards my bedroom and yelled, "You gonna have sex in my bed, get caught and tell me no I can't leave?" I must say, I yelled a little more than that, words that you cannot imagine. The words I yelled to Derrick pissed him off and he got angry and said to me "You not going anywhere" and even had the nerve to ask me why was I home so early anyway. My mind went blank and I jumped on him and begin to punch him continuously. He somehow grabbed a hold of me and held me down. He told me to calm down and I somehow got the strength to move him off of me. As soon as I had him off of me, I ran to tackle the woman who he had been sleeping with. I wanted to kill somebody that day. The apartment was filled with yelling and crying, but in the middle of all the chaos, I remember hearing nothing but Elijah and his cry brought me back to reality.

I grabbed him and locked us up in the bedroom. As I grabbed the car seat with Elijah in it I looked in to make sure he was okay because I heard him crying but to my disbelief, he was sound asleep. I put him in his bassinet and I sat on the floor. I wanted to cry but I sat there numb, feeling like there is no way out of this hell. As I sat on the floor, I looked over to where the T.V was and I saw a bottle of pills. As I crawled over to get the pills and open the bottle, I heard Elijah yarn and I dropped the pills I had on the floor. I began to cry like a little baby. I couldn't believe that I had wanted to kill myself just to get out of this hell, I wanted my mommy, I wanted my daddy. I was angry, I was hurt, I was alone, I was confused and most of all I felt trapped. These feeling consumed me and I could not explain the pain and hurt that I was feeling. To walk in and see what I saw and feel trapped because this guy would not release me. I was in hell. I mean really, I'm thinking what else could possibly happen now. For the next couple of days, it was quiet in the house. Derrick wasn't saying much to me and I wasn't talking to him at all. I wouldn't even let him come near Elijah. I was sleeping on the floor because it disgusted me to be on the bed. I wanted to take a knife and cut the bed up but I didn't want to be sued by the rental office, the apartment was in my name, so I left that idea alone.

Out of the blue, Derrick busted into the room and yelled, "Look I'm not scared of you, you are not going to have me up all night, you got them shook but you better not touch them!" I replied very calm, "You better not leave them alone with me then," then I continued to play with my baby. I was hurt and I was determined to hurt all those who played a part in hurting me. After for about a month, he had not left the house as far as going to make the girls work. At night, he would sleep in the living room and I would lock the door and sleep on the floor. But one night, I had to use the bathroom so I got up and opened the door to go to the bathroom. As I walked passed, in the living room I could see the same prostitute put his penis back in his underwear. I looked and he looked back at me and said, "Man Angel, ain't nobody doing nothing." At this time, I was so tired and didn't know what to do, I replied, "Yeah sure, I don't even care, do ya'll need the bedroom again?" and went to the bathroom. As the funds begun to get short, he started to get upset and kept making comments about me staying. He kept apologizing and telling me not to leave, but everything he said went in one ear and right out of the other. The thing is in the middle of his craziness towards me he would make comments about my parents and I believed him because of the hell I was going through. I would hear the horror stories that him and his friends laughed about and I knew he was a heartless person so I did not believe his threats were threats but I believed he would do what he promised.

I heard someone once say that fear can consume you and I have to strongly agree because at this point of my life, fear was currently consuming me. My old Bible class teacher in North Carolina said that fear stood for, False Elusions Appearing Real. In today's society, we get consumed over the "What if's" or the "Maybe's" but in Jesus Christ we have an anchor and we do not have to be afraid of what man say they can do to us. People get afraid of false evidence and live in fear that is caused by mind wars. We must be able to confront fear with the Word of God and face it head on. We must let fear know that you know what's real and you know who controls the destiny of your life. At this time in my life, I was consumed with so much hurt and fear. After I got pregnant, I found out that Derrick's mom was into Voodoo and she would pay money to go see a man who truly really believed that what he was doing was working against me and this same lady proclaimed to be a Christian. I allowed the enemy to use fear to have control over me. I also allowed the enemy to consume me, overwhelm me and keep me trapped in fear of the "what if's". I didn't quite understand the scripture that says, "For God has not given us the spirit of fear, but of power and of love and of a sound mind" 2 Timothy 1:7 KJV. I didn't understand that fear was a spirit and that the spirit I should have been filled with was the Holy Spirit. I should have had that love of God, that power of God and that sounded mind to hear God.

The enemy knows exactly what to do to distract you and knock you off post. The enemy knows he already lost but he still wants to devour the people of God, especially those with callings and gifts. I know things happen in our life that causes us to wake up and say enough is enough or it can make you throw in the towel and give up. If we are still alive then God has a plan for us. Know this beloved, that the enemy comes to kill, steal, and destroy. He wants to kill your ministry, steal your joy, and destroy your life. He does not want your possessions, money or your spouse and loved ones but he wants your joy because he knows that the joy of the Lord is your strength. We are set apart for God's use; and although things have happened to you either bad or the worst, our Savior can and will turn that thing around for your good. That's the Word of God. Jesus has a wonderful plan for our lives. He promises us life and life more abundantly. That's what we have to hold on to in our storms. We have to take responsibility for our actions, meaning take responsibility in how we react to the situations or storms of life. When I look back through the years, it is wonderful how he kept me but I also realized that I could have handle things differently or been more obedient. God placed certain people in my life to listen to and I should have been where I was supposed to be instead of allowing the enemy to steal my foundation away. We have so many promises in the Word of God and they are already inside us but we have to activate them by studying the Word of God and understanding who we belong to. If I would have known a quarter of what I know now, I would not have allowed the enemy to control me for so long and burden me with so much pain.

I chose not to leave Derrick of course for several reasons. First because we had a son together and I did not want to raise my son without a father and second because even through the heartache and pain I thought I had some love for him or I was scared to be alone. I would pray for deliverance and for a way out of my hell or that he would change his ways and that I would be enough for him. I know now, a man will not change unless he wants to. There was no change. He thought because he bought me J-Lo jump suits, Gucci bags, matching shoes and other designer things that I was supposed to be happy with that. But I was not happy because I just wanted him and wanted him to have only better characteristics. Even with all the hell I was going through, I still didn't like to see him go through. One day he went out town to Georgia where some of his family had lived. He claimed that everything was going good and he was not doing anything wrong while he was away. When he returned however, he had many guns with him. As he took them out of his bag to clean them, he pointed one at my head. As he played around, the gun went off and the bullet flew right by head. Derrick begun to laugh as he made a crazy joke about it almost hitting me and joking about what if our baby was

67

walking by at the time the gun went off. He would say the craziest and scariest things; he had an evil sense of humor. As the days went by, I finally found out what was really going on in Georgia or what he said was going on. Derrick got himself into some legal trouble and the state of Georgia was after him. His side of the story was that he purchased guns from a local Pawn store legally and although he purchased them legally, the state of Georgia was charging him with gun trafficking. Derrick and his mom was doing all they could to try to beat this case against him.

One day, I was out with my mom and I noticed that my cell phone did not ring at all that day which was not normal because he kept close tabs on me. As I dropped my mom off and headed home, I decided to give him a call but the phone went straight to voicemail. Then I remembered that his mom was hospitalized at the time due to an illness, so I just assumed that he was there visiting her. As I pulled up into our apartment complex, I saw police officers in black uniforms everywhere. I parked and quickly walked to my apartment building because I knew something crazy was getting ready to happen to someone but never in my wildest dreams would I have thought that person would be me. I continued up the steps quickly and went inside my apartment. I decided to place Elijah in the bed and call my mom because I had a gut feeling something was not right and she told me she would be right over. As I waited for my mother to arrive, there was a knock on my door. I opened the door and was greeted by a detective dressed in a suit, he explained who and what he was looking for. He continued to talk, and while he was talking, I noticed my mom outside, and at first they would not allow her to come into the building. She fussed with a few officers and they finally decided to let her in. The detective begin explaining to my mom what was going on until another police officer interrupted and whispered to him, "We got him sir." I looked at the officer's face and I knew they had finally had him in custody. Derrick had hid the guns and had stated that only three people knew where they were but somehow the ATF knew exactly where to look as if somebody told them the location of each one. My mommy asked me to go home with her that night but I told her that I just honestly wanted to be alone.

My mind was racing and I had so many thoughts in my head; do I leave now or do I wait, will this change him, is this really happening and I just want to be left alone. The next day, Derrick called collect and told me what happened. He said as he was walking out from seeing his mom they arrested him and because he was unable to post bail, he had to sit there and wait until the state of Georgia came to get him. I did not know how long he was going to be locked up so I just tried my best to stay on his good side and even took the time out to visit him the entire time. Although Derrick was in jail, he was still controlling. When he called the first time and I didn't answer, he would keep calling back to back until I picked up. When I finally was able to answer, he would yell all types of things at me like, what am I doing, am I cheating, you not going to stay by my side and so on. Since he was still being held in D.C. jail, I would visit him and stay by the phone just in case he called which he always did. For the next month and a half, he stayed in D.C. jail until they finally released him on house arrest because Georgia did not make a decision on what they wanted to do with him. While he was on house arrest, he had to stay with his dad because his dad paid his bail and they released him into his custody. Derrick forced Elijah and me to come to stay there with him as well so he could keep an eye on me. While his dad was home, Derrick would not act up or do the normal things he would do but when his dad left, that was another story. During the time I stayed with his family, his mom would always have somewhere to go, something to do and always wanted me to drive her around, which I didn't mind because I was helping her. Little did I know was that she was actually getting me out of the house so that Derrick could have company, other females over and work on his so-called music.

One day, we went to the flea market and as we were on our way back, she called him and used her little code words to tell him that we were on our way back. I was so sick of them two thinking I was stupid and didn't know what was going on. I yelled, "Whoever is over there, make her stay in the apartment with y'all and let me go home and be about my business!" Cheryl said, "Stop that Angel ain't nobody over there." I continued to talk and told her I was not dumb, I know their little games and what he is doing. Why would he keep me in all this drama when he is free to do what he wants and without

71

argument? He should just let me leave; but nobody seen it my way, I was just stuck. We pulled up to his dad's house and he had an attitude but so did I. I walked passed him and we did not say a word to each other. I watched T.V and he stayed locked up in the bedroom. When his dad came home, he told Cheryl to freshen up because they were going out to eat. After they left, I took Elijah in the living room with me. We stayed in the living room and watched T.V and played for about three hours without Derrick even attempting to come out of his room or say anything to me. Finally Derrick had enough and busted out of the room and started fussing with me. He called me all types of dumb this and stupid that but I ignored him and that made him angrier. As I continued to ignore him, he grabbed me and pulled me in the room, while Elijah was in his bouncy, vibrating chair. He kept asking me "What's wrong with you, how you gonna try and leave me now at a time like this?" With a smirk I replied, "It's ok for you to treat me like crap and continue to cheat on me and I'm supposed to just sit back, take it and do nothing, yeah ok, whatever." Derrick took that as me saying I was going to cheat on him because he yelled, "What, you gonna cheat on me now?" I knew where this was heading because he would take the littlest thing and make it so huge. As I walked away, Derrick continued to yell vulgar things and then he got in my face as if he was going to hit me. I knew the punches were coming, so I told myself to prepare for them. I don't know what happened but I all of a sudden could not breathe. It felt like I was having an asthma attack and Derrick was just looking at me and starring. I was crying, my heart was beating really fast, I could not see and I did not know what was going on. I just kept fighting for air. I could hear him yelling, "Stop that, stop that, man if you die in here, breathe, stop that!" as if I could control what was going on.

As his mom and dad walked back in the house from dinner, he yelled for them to come get me. His father asked him what happened and his mom ran to get a cold wash cloth. She put the wash cloth on me and said very calmly, "slowly breathe; no one in here is going to hurt you, slowly breathe, calm down Angel, its ok." After a few moments, I started to breathe normal but I was really tired and thirsty. I had made myself have a panic attack. I was panicking over something that had not yet happened. I feared something that had not yet come to pass. I thought I was preparing myself but I ended up harming myself.

IS HELL ABOUT TO BE OVER?

A month passed and it was time for Derrick to go to court. The state of Georgia decided to come get him from D.C. I stayed home to take care of Elijah and I continued to go through all types of emotions. It was finally peaceful in the house and I was able to come and go as I pleased but I ensured that I didn't miss his phone calls because it would only cause him to yell. Day after day, I had begun to feel sad because I was lonely. I would often think how could I move on with my life, I have a child and I was ugly, I felt low. My self-esteem was gone and my life was gone. I was going through all types of mind wars. The only joy I really had was my son. I would take care of him and show him all my love. One day, we traveled to Georgia for Derrick's final trial and we stayed with his grandma. Her home was hot and miserable. The day of the trial everything moved very slowly. I was not able to go in the court room because I had the baby. After hours and hours of waiting, the court sentenced him to two years. Once dismissed, he walked out of the courtroom first accompanied by police officers and was handcuffed. He looked over at me and shook his head in sorrow, I felt his pain. I cried and was very emotional. I had many thoughts in my head. They sent him to serve his time in Cumberland Prison. In the beginning, I would go to see him often. Sometimes I would stay in the hotel so I could see him Saturday and Sunday for his entire visitation time. A few times during our visits, he would have an attitude, get up, walk away and go back to his cell. I understand he was upset but I traveled with a baby through the mountains for three hours and he had the nerve to walk away and go back to his cell.

Other times the visits were nice and calm. We would laugh and just enjoy each other's company. He would tell me how much he missed me and how he was going to change when he got home. He would make so many promises; he said he was not going to cheat, lie or pimp anymore. I believed him at first until it came time for me to find a job. I decided to give up the apartment because I was not working and could not afford it alone. I moved in with my mom and began to look for a job and seek help from the state. When I found a job and began to work, Derrick did not like that. He thought I was cheating and not working. It was his guilt eating at him. When I got paid it wasn't enough to even pay child care. As I began to work and get myself together, I was slowly letting go of Derrick. I would ignore his calls and focus on just moving on with my life. I started to ignore the phone calls because I had a lot on my plate and did not want to have to explain my every move and hear a grown man question me, I was tired. Eventually, the phone calls and letters stopped. I finally was free. I was coming to myself. I finally got tired of that low paying job and I quit. I would walk into different buildings and apply for jobs and I also went to the Employment office and apply for jobs. I was determined to find a good job. One day, I got up once again and took Elijah to the daycare and I walked the mall. I went in one store and asked if they were hiring. The manger stated, "Yes we are. What position did you want to apply for?" "A sales associate," I replied very low and timid. She took my resume and said "No, you are too qualified, we need an Assistant Manager, and I'm going to interview you for that." I was so shock and so happy that I didn't know what to do. I told my mom and days later I was hired as an Assistant Manager for that clothing store.

I was working, I had my child in daycare and I was feeling independent again. I got a new car, and was saving money so that I would be able to move out on my own again.

A year and a half passed and I was making it and really happy about finding myself again as a woman. I had made new friends and had a life again. Working at the clothing store opened the door for me to get a new job with better pay and later helped me achieve a great career path working for a bank. I was able to save and pay for daycare. I wasn't making a whole lot of money but I was getting back on top of things. I was able to take care of my son and I with some left over. Shortly after me accepting my new job, it was also time for Derrick to get out of jail. I slowly started to once again take his calls and we started talking. He talked about and made more and more promises. In my mind, I thought he changed and things would be different and that he realized I was all he needed. I just knew that he saw that everyone had turned their backs on him and that I was the only true friend and woman he had. He was getting released and he asked me to come pick him up. I said yes and went to Cumberland to pick him up. For a moment it was nice, no arguing, no fighting. It was great to hear him say he missed me and loved me and that he wanted his family back. It was great to hear him promise he would not mess up again. I ate up everything he said like chocolate and I put my guards down and let him back in. I took him to the half-way house and I would visit him during visitation hours or come see him during his breaks. I would bring Elijah to go see him as well. The first month was okay and then I started to notice his mom talking in codes again. UGH, he we go again. I couldn't believe it.

I know by now many of you reading this is thinking, "She is stupid, what's her problem and why she stay in it and kept dealing with him." Well I have to be honest, it was not all bad. I loved that man and would have done anything for him. In the midst of the chaos, at times we had fun enjoying each other. I absolutely love seafood, so he would bring home bushels of seafood and we would have our own feast and watch movies. We really did not go out much but something had a stronghold on me when it came to that man. About a month in the halfway house, I seen his mom going back to her old tricks which meant her son too was back to his. She would drop off money that some prostitutes gave her to give to him. Was she serious? When I knew for a fact that this was going on, I anxiously waited for his phone call. The phone finally rung and I answered yelling, "You got to be kidding me man, you still up to no good!" "Stop yelling Angel, I know better now not to let them in the house, they not going to bother us, somebody else driving them around and all I have to do is meet up with them and collect money. Baby I don't have a job and I have to pay bills." Then it clicked in my head, pay bills? He was in a halfway house and I had got a new apartment. He had already assumed he was moving in the apartment with me. I was the one who got an apartment and was paying rent and going to work. I really had not planned for him to join me so soon. I replied, "So you think you moving in?" "Angel stop playing, yes I am, you my woman" and as stupid as it sounds, I let him back in. He promised and promised that he would find a job and leave that life alone and I believed. Promises, promises, promises.

If you let your guard down and let the enemy in, that's when he will try his hardest to kill, steal and destroy you. The Word of God tells us about the enemy's resume.

The Word of God warns us about the enemy and his workers of iniquity. Your joy and salvation is what the enemy wants from you. In John 10:10 KJV it says, "The thief cometh not, but for to steal, and to kill, and to destroy: I am come that they might have life, and that they might have [it] more abundantly." One thing you have to keep in mind; when God delivers you from something, it's for a reason. The reason being is that whatever or whoever it is does not mean us any good. God knows that it is not right for our spirit and He knows that He has the best for us. I prayed and prayed for God to get me out the situation drama free. I wanted the Lord to grant me a peaceful separation. I was so blind that I was unable to see that the Lord did just as I had asked. He granted me favor and I did have a peaceful separation without all the drama but because I was weak minded, I allowed Derrick and all of the drama to come back into my life. God had wanted me to just leave him alone but I didn't. Since I did not pass the test and I did not learn my lesson the first time around, the Lord had to make sure that when He delivered me from this man again, I would finally learn my lesson and not get back into a relationship with him again. The first time around was just the storm for me but the second time around was the lesson I was going to learn during the storm.

Time went on and I felt in my heart that Derrick was slowly going back to his old ways after coming home from the halfway house. He was staying out late, drinking and all. This time he did not bring the prostitutes home but he would just stay out with them. I knew what was going on but I just dealt with it and kept my distance. He had been home for about a month and had not physically abused me but emotionally, there was a lot of name calling and putting me down. So much for him saying he really missed me. I had a good job, so it helped to drown myself in work and take care of Elijah to pass the time. When my birthday arrived, I decided to try and take the week off if the job permitted me to. On the night before my birthday, I was sitting alone in the house and I began to see visions of what Derrick was doing out there. He arrived to the house about 7:00 am the next morning as I was lying in bed. I didn't say anything to him because I just want to keep the peace. He started to hang pictures in the living room and fix the place up. His phone kept vibrating so I finally gave in and rolled over to pick it up but couldn't figure out how to work it. I had no intention of trying to snoop through his phone. When I figured the phone out it went straight to the videos. I saw a video dated for July 8 at 3:15am and I want to know what it was because I wondered what he would be recording at 3am that morning.

I proceeded to open the video and to my surprise it was a female giving him oral sex, on my birthday. I had so many thoughts and so much pain running through me. I let this guy back in my house and most importantly my heart. He betrayed me again. I couldn't explain how hurt my feelings were, I couldn't explain how disrespected I felt, I couldn't explain how badly I wanted this pain to end. But God reminded me that I had an angel of my own and that I had a purpose. At that time, I simply thought my purpose was to take care of Elijah. When I saw the video on the phone, I stopped breathing and the room was spinning. So much darkness overcame me and the room seemed dimmed. I made sure Elijah was sleeping and then I grabbed the cell phone, went in the living room and threw it at his head. It hit the wall and I yelled, "You lying no good devil. How dare you do this to me again, after I waited for you and let you back in my heart. You just want to hurt me, why are you trying to kill me?" He stated, "What's wrong with you? What you find now? Stop being nosey!" "Stop being nosey, are you serious? You have a female licking on you and your response is stop being nosey? Just get out! Get out", I yelled hysterically. He just looked at me and laughed. He walked over to me and tried to hug me as he brushed it off as a joke. I pushed him off, picked up his phone and gave it to him so he could see what I had already seen.

I looked at his face as he watched the video and he was shocked. He sat there with his mouth opened and did not utter a word. I folded my arms and then calmly said get out. He said I'm sorry and I love you so many times as if that was going to take the pain I was feeling away. I was devastated and felt like I couldn't take anymore. Derrick left out of the house with no physical fight, which was really shocking. After he left, I grabbed some of my things and I left with Elijah to move in with my dad. I had still been hiding the abuse I was suffering because I was still so ashamed to talk about it. When we moved in with my dad, he did not ask questions or judge, he just let me stay. Every other day I would go to the apartment to visit mainly for Elijah but really for me. I still wanted Derrick. I just wanted to be able to say that I had a man or my child was brought up with both parents. One day, I was relaxing at my dad's house and Derrick called and said we needed to talk. Thinking nothing of it, I got myself and Elijah dressed and I went over to the apartment. I arrived before him and decided to go in the bedroom and watch T.V. until he came home. When he arrived home, he walked in and yelled my name, "Angel!" and I remember him sounding demonic and a fear coming over me because of the unknown of what he was angry about all of a sudden. He took the baby and laid him in the other room as I just sat there... just starring. I asked what was wrong with him and he went off. He was yelling and calling me all types of degrading names. He was accusing me of cheating and repeatedly degrading me and whatever degrading name you can think of, he was calling me just that. Come to find out, he went to the doctor and found out that he had an STD. I screamed. How dare he even blame me? Me, I was faithful, I was honest with him and I wasn't with anyone else but him. I couldn't even think and care about who gave him a STD but I was more concerned with the possibility of me now having it. All types of thoughts and things were going through my head. While he continued fussing, I blacked out and vomited everywhere. My emotions could not handle all the pressure. To make that situation worst after I got myself together, he grabbed me and threw me on the bed.

He held my face and pinned me down on the bed so he could begin to break me down. He went right to my ear and said, "You know what Angel, you are nothing, you are nasty, you stink, nobody will ever want you or love you, and you're not even that pretty anyway. All you have is a nice body and that's all men want from you is your body." He said way more than that, but because the stuff was extremely vulgar I will leave it out. As he was talking, I was slowly dying. He was destroying my spirit and through him, the enemy was planting death seeds. I was so hurt by the words he was saying. I know growing up it was taught that sticks and stones may break my bones but words will never hurt me, but this is one the most untrue statements. Words can kill you and the words that were being said to me was killing me, destroying my very being. It was like he was doing it on purpose; he went straight to my ears and held me down so I can hear him. The comments he was saying was as if he wanted me to take a gun and kill myself mainly because in his statements he mentioned I should kill myself because I was worthless. After what seemed like forever, he finally got up and left me there crying. I was balled up in the fetal position just crying and crying.

I heard the door slam and I was there just crying. I mustered up enough strength to get Elijah, feed him and lay him in the bed next to me. I couldn't drive back to my dad's and I was exhausted. I thought it was over; he had succeeded in making me feel even less than the slum of the earth. He destroyed my spirit more than he ever had, but little did I know; hell was not over. I was lying in the bed and the sounds of the front door slamming awakened me. He came into the apartment with his cousin and some other female. He instantly came running in the room in one of his rages again, fussing and yelling about nothing. He was saying that I made him sick and he was done with me. I told him that was fine, just stop yelling because he had woken Elijah up. He started yelling at me and jumping in my face in front of Elijah. I just wanted to calm him down because I was trying to comfort my son; I could see that my son was frightened by his actions. I knew for sure he was back to his normal self. He got in my face and yelled while balling his fist up as if he was going to hit me. I yelled, "Stop! You are scaring my baby!" Truth be told he was scaring me too but he didn't care. I have no remembrance on what was said until the next day. As Elijah was in the backseat playing with his toy he reenacted the whole situation from the night before. I heard my son say, "Stop Derrick, you're scaring my baby", then he yelled in a deep man's voice (as deep as his little voice could get), "Shut up Whore, I don't care!. When I heard those words, I realized what was trying to take place even then; I knew right then I had to leave. I knew I had to take my baby and never look back. I was determined not to raise another man to grow up and think it was okay to beat up on women for any reason. I knew that I had to what I call now, reveal my wound. I had to tell the secrets and open the sores to make sure my baby lived. To show that I was serious about leaving Derrick, I had to tell my parents everything. If I really wanted to get out of this hell, I knew I would have to start opening my mouth and seek help. I knew that I needed help because I could not do it on my own.

The devil knows how to keep people in bondage and keep them in slavery in their minds. If you are around evil and do not have the foundation of Jesus Christ, then it's easy for you to think something as evil as beating on women is acceptable. There are women who actually think when her man shows a jealous rage and/or hit her that he loves her. The devil is liar because love does not beat you in the face until you can't recognize yourself. Love does not try to kill you with words. The Word of God says "Love is patient, love is kind. It does not envy, it does not boast, it is not proud. [5] It does not dishonor others, it is not self-seeking, it is not easily angered, it keeps no record of wrongs. [6] Love does not delight in evil but rejoices with the truth. [7] It always protects, always trusts, always hopes, and always perseveres." 1 Corinthians 13:4-7 KJV I was not going to allow that stronghold and curse continue in my child. It was time to put action behind my decision. I dropped Elijah off at his grandmother's house and I went back to the apartment where I and Derrick stayed and I grabbed as much clothes as I could. Then I wrote a letter and I left it on his keyboard. When I was done I left and went to my dad's house and I told my dad what was going on, all about the abuse and how I was determined to not go back. I got a protective order against Derrick and it did not work. He stalked me on my job and my dad's house. He would call my work phone and hang up. If I answered, he would yell in the phone and call me names. He would tell me how I wore my hair and what I had on that day. He vandalized my car by putting some type of juice or diesel gas into the gas tank. When I called the police, nothing happened because they had no real evidence. I was starting to understand why so many women were in prison because the system was failing to protect them. Some women felt like in order to survive, they had to take matters into their own hands even if it meant losing their freedom and I felt the same way. I was ready to lose my freedom but as I looked over at my angel, I heard a voice say "And where would that leave your baby?" All I could do was weep uncontrollably. I wanted to be free from this man but I did not want to lose my child. I did not want my child to grow without a mother and father behind me doing things my way and not trusting in God.

I knew in order for me to live a "normal" life that I may have to relocate but I was trying to prepare myself for a move. Well the enemy did not like that I was trying to have peace in my life.

SEEING DEATH BEFORE HER EYES

—————————— ∘❦❦∘ ——————————

One morning I got a very disturbing phone call from Cheryl. She was going on and on about how she couldn't believe that I had a protective order against her son because he is Elijah's dad. She went on to say that the abuse he put me though was not that serious. I couldn't believe my ears, I thought to myself, lady your son would beat me until I couldn't even recognize myself. You never thought that it was that serious. She stayed on the phone and continued to fuss and yell at me as I tuned her out. I arrived at my son's grandmother's house and I took the key out the ignition and locked the door. It was like God was telling me something because on a normal day, I would leave my key in the ignition and run Elijah to his grandmother (this grandmother that I speak of is a lady who adopted us in her family as if we were blood) at the door. I picked my son up and held the cell phone in my hand as Cheryl continued arguing. I walked to her porch and a young lady with a black bubble coat, short jeans, black K-Swiss tennis shoes with no socks and ashy ankles, walked pass me. She walked right pass me, so close that we almost bumped. I chose not to pay her any attention. Usually after I ran the baby to the porch, I would run back to the car but today I didn't do that. I sat on Elijah's grandmother's porch and talked to Cheryl on the phone for about 3 minutes. I slowly walked back to my mom's car, I had to borrow her car because mine had been vandalized.

As I walking to the car the same female that walked passed me came back around and ran towards me with a yellow cup in her hand. Out of nowhere, she threw some type of liquid substance on me, with the intentions on throwing it on my face; all I could do was turn around and run. I ran up the street because she was chasing me but then I heard the cup fall so I stop running and turned around to fight and chase her. We ran up the hill and as I was chasing her, I felt something drip on my coat. I panicked and ran back to my son's grandmother house. I realized that I still had my cell phone in my hand and Cheryl was still on the phone. I put the phone to my ear and I heard her say, "What, what's wrong, we didn't do anything!" She said this before I could say anything. I yelled, "You two are going to jail today!" I hung up on her and I called the police. While waiting for the police to come, I ran into grandma's house and started to take my clothes off and cut my hair because I had no idea of what the liquid substance was. The police finally arrived with hazmat, an ambulance and the FBI. They blocked off the whole street for about five blocks to test the substance and ensure that no one got in or out. I was questioned over and over again by the detective and I explained to him on why I left and why I thought Derrick and his mom had something to do with this incident.

The guy from Hazmat came over to the car and said that the substance that was thrown at me was some type of acid that commercial cleaners use to sometimes burn the deep dirt grud off. He explained that they have to wear special gloves and protection because if it touches a person's skin it would burn them. The Hazmat tech said that it will burn through a person's skin. The only thing I could do was cry and think; what if she was crazy enough to throw that acid on me while I had my son because she did walk right pass me while I was holding him. What would she have done if the acid would have hit me in the face? I thank God that death nor harm touched me but then at the time I was thinking of the "what if's". Due to the new information the detective received about the substance he said that if proven Derrick had something to do with it he would be charged with attempted murder. Murder, at that time all I could do was think about how I just wanted to be happy and free from an abusive man yet he wanted to murder me because of it. That day I lived in fear and constantly watched my back. I was terrified. I called my employer and explained what had happened and they gave me the day off.

TRYING TO CLOSE

THIS CHAPTER OF HELL

I went to work that day just to let them know I had to leave. I explained to my managers what was going on, which they already knew. They knew that the phone calls that constantly came through with someone hanging up was him. I had to explain to them that I could not focus or even work and I had to go away. I was seconds away from being murdered and I was now able to see how God's hand was and still is over my life but at that time I was far from thanking God and I allowed the enemy to cover me in fear. After I left the job, I had to quickly make arrangements with my son's grandmother. I wanted to take him with me but my parent's and Elijah's grandmother thought that it was best that I go and get my mind together. They told me that once I was able to get myself settled then I would be able to come back and get my baby. I was hurt in a way that I could not even explain. Someone tried to violently hurt and kill me and now I had to leave my child behind because I was not mentally stable to take care of him. Weeks went by and it was time to go to court and for me to pick up my son. Travelling back towards home, I was so paranoid. I constantly thought I was being followed. I thought Derrick was in the shadows and that frightened me.

We went to court the next morning after I arrived to Maryland. That day, my mom, my son, me and a friend of mine at the time, went to court because of the protective order. I remembered being in court waiting and looking around because I just knew Derrick was going to try something crazy; and he did. In the court room, he kept looking at me and I looked back at him. He then walked up to my male friend and tapped him on the shoulder. He asked him if he could see him outside for a minute. Derrick's friends grabbed him and told him, "Not in here man"; so he walked away. As we were in court, Derrick pretended to fall out in the court house and his mother started screaming "Call the ambulance; he had a massive heart attack before, help him!" The police put me, my mom, my son and the guy in the room until they left. The judge said that the court date had to be postponed due to the incident. As we were leaving the building, I looked over my shoulder and looked around at other cars. I just knew this man was following me but I decided to go back to North Carolina that night with my son. When I arrived, I thought I had left everything behind in Maryland but little did I know I was so wrong.

THE MENTAL HELL

I travelled to North Carolina that day to stay with some family members there. I had not told them what exactly was going on other than I wanted a change and needed to get away from my son's father but they had very little details; at least that was what I thought. When I arrived, a cousin of mine offered for me to stay with her, but her invitation was not as welcoming as I thought it would have been. She explained to me that I could stay with her until her husband came home in about a month but then I would have to have a job because I would have to leave. This made me feel very uncomfortable and I just wanted to really leave.

How many of you know that the devil can come in sheep clothing trying to play the hero. A family friend stepped in and helped me out. He would get off of work about 5:00 am, take a nap and have me out the house by 8:00 am so I could look for a job. When I wanted to get away from family and just be alone, he would allow me to stay at his apartment in quiet where I was able to cry to myself or just rest. I couldn't believe that here I was; in another state, away from my mommy and my daddy. I was hurt and lonely. I couldn't figure out why Elijah's dad hated me so much, I didn't understand how I lost myself, how I had gotten into a crazy abusive relationship, how my life was upside down and how I lost control of it all. I started to recognize that this family friend was helping me and also feeding me lines of how stupid the other guy was for letting me go and how he would never hurt me or do me wrong. This man would say all the right things and it made me feel special. I finally felt like I was worthy to be happy. He made me a promise, a promise to make me happy and never hurt me. I was a young woman who was already wounded, hurt and bleeding but he was willing to take my weak broken heart and I gave it to him. I felt safe with him and really thought that he was God sent, but wait a minute, how could I think this man was God sent and I wasn't even seeking God? As weeks went by, I eventually moved in with this man. I was looking for daycares and I was able to find a job that would help pay some bills and daycare. I felt like I was finally happy again. I thought that I had control of my life. In six weeks I had fell in love and got myself together again.

Each morning, I would get up, get Elijah up, feed him breakfast, get him to daycare and go to work. After work, I would pick my son up from daycare, cook dinner, put my son to bed, the cry myself to sleep. Then the next day, I would do it all over again. I was working in a warehouse as a temporary Admin Assistant. Although it was a temporary position, I was able to get my boyfriend a full-time permanent position with the company. We worked for the same company, in the same building but I worked in the front office and he worked in the warehouse part. With the warehouse being so big, I was always so jumpy every time someone opened the door to the office I was in. I was not able to go to company mass meetings in the warehouse because I was afraid and paranoid. I just could not take being around large crowds of people. I was afraid and terrified. I would believe that I saw Derrick in the building and almost everywhere I was. One morning I had to take my boyfriend to work because we had one car and he had to be to work before me. As I was driving to drop him off, I thought I saw Derrick. I was so sure that was him even until this day. I saw a clear picture of his face and it was his car parked on the side of the road early that morning. This caused me to once again start looking around and checking out my surroundings all the time. People with masks or even motorcycle helmets could not be around me without me freaking out. On my way home that same day, I was at a stop light and looked over to my right and I saw him on the phone outside his car talking. It was him but the only person that saw him was me. I called my boyfriend and he told me that he thought I was just seeing things. I went home and cried. I started talking to myself and answering myself. I literally felt like I was losing my mind.

Many days, my cell phone would ring with strange numbers appearing but when I answered; no one would say a word. Then shortly after, my house phone would ring and still no one would say a word when I answered. I thought I was being harassed but my boyfriend just told me I was losing my mind. It got so bad that I had to take my son to his grandmother's house so that I could relax but I couldn't, my mind was playing tricks on me. I remember waking up one morning and I literally could not walk. When I look down I was swollen with hives. My legs and arms were red and swollen too; so I went to the emergency room and the nurse claimed that it was only my nerves. Stress was causing me to break out in hives. Finally, my mom convinced me to see a therapist. I went to the therapist and she referred me to a psychiatrist. One week I would speak with the therapist and the next week was the psychiatrist. I thought it was terrible. The psychiatrist said that I was hallucinating and paranoid, she diagnosed me with PTSS (Post Traumatic Stress Syndrome). She stated that in my mind I was in a war and no one could be trusted. My mind made me believe that everyone was out to get me and that's exactly how I felt. She prescribed medicine that didn't work, so she kept increasing my dosage. Then she decided to change the type of medicine I was taking but I just kept crying and throwing fits.

I was mentally unstable and making myself physically sick. I was mentally ill and had been hospitalized because of stress, seeing things, hearing things; and the fact that I was not able to be around crowds of people, I became miserable. I was dealing with so much that I just wanted to die. I felt like if I had received one bad move or sign of drama, I was going to terminate my life. This caused so much unnecessary drama to go on between me and my boyfriend at the time. One late night, I was at the park watching the water and I could hear the devil telling me to jump. But the Holy Ghost was saying that's not my Will, then the enemy would say but no one loves you and then I heard my friend's country voice yell "You're going to hell!" Well that made me drive away; at this point I didn't know what to believe or what to do about anything. I remember sitting at home and looking at the Bible, just starring at it. I could remember being younger and in church and how sometimes those were happy days for me when I wasn't being sneaky. I said to myself if I felt that kind of peace then, what would I feel now as a broken woman? I picked up the Bible and started reading it. I would complete books at a time and I felt lighter and lighter. I kept going to my doctor and the therapist. I even continued taking the medicine. One day I decided to take a step further and I went back to church. I was enjoying myself and starting to get my happy back. I was also getting back the joy of the Lord. Situations around me didn't change but my mind and my attitude did; which made the difference. So much supernatural things were happening to me; I was having personal conversations with Jesus and could clearly hear

His voice. One day I woke and I said, "No more!". I meant no more medicine and no more depression and no more meetings or doctor's appointments. I stopped my medicine cold turkey and was fine. Some days I felt like screaming and crying but then I would pray and before a tear fell, I would praise my sadness into gladness. The doctor did not recommend me to stop that way but I clearly told her my faith was stronger and I am healed. She kept trying to get me to lower dosage and not just stop completely but I stood strong to my faith and knew God was able to heal and He did. When I made up my mind I did not take another pill or go to another meeting. I was healed. Troubles were still apparent in my relationship and my finances but I was handling it better with the help of Jesus. I was faithful to my church and enjoying Jesus. I was listening to Him and He was revealing visions and talking to me through them. He revealed good and not so good things and was just enjoying ministry. I knew what it was to have the joy of the Lord even in the chaos that was still around me.

I knew I was healed for a fact. I remember one night I was in the house alone. I was reading my Bible and my house phone rang, I answered, "Hello", the guy replied "Yeah chick, I got your house number so you know I got your address!" I replied calmly, "Yes that maybe true, soooo what exactly do you want again?" He responded in anger, he went off yelling how he was a gorilla pimp and would knock my head off and how he was getting ready to come to my door steps. I waited until he was done and I laughed. I calmly replied, "Well man, if you are so bad and bigger than my God, I dare you to knock on this door. I dare you to even step foot on my door step. I serve a God that is bigger, stronger and protecting me. He won't let you harm me, but if you don't believe me by all means you are welcome to step on my front porch." After that it was no response and he hung up. Right then I knew my fear of Derrick was gone and I was safe in Jesus.

HAPPY DAYS TRYING TO UNCOVER

Well time has passed and it's known that I am dating this guy. This guy has a past but I don't judge people on their past I find the good in all people. I can't say that he was all bad just that we both had issues at the time we were together and it was terrible. I met him of course while going through drama with Derrick, so this guy made me feel secure. I felt protected. He would travel with me back and forth to Maryland and would help me with my son, at times. I learned that this man just wanted to be free. I was already embarrassed because of the stuff that I was going through so I dare not show unhappiness with the new guy, right.

But behind those closed doors; I was dealing with a cheating man who thought all women were crazy, although never physically abusive he was verbally abusive; he had no respect for women not even his own mother according to the things he would say; he would call his mom and sisters crazy. He had a deep hurt from his mom and therefore categorized all women the same. To add to the mental confusion he had of women, his cheating also lead him to have a baby with another woman while we were together and me being stalked by the husband of his mistress. Yes, I was stalked by the husband of the woman this guy chose to cheat with. What did I have to do with it, nothing. Just know that I came to my senses and realized that I am loved by Christ Jesus and I don't have to be in a bad relationship or marriage. I was dealing with too much that I didn't have to be is this relationship. The name calling, the disrespect of my gift and having a baby outside of our relationship caused so much pain. I know that I am a jewel and I am fearfully and wonderfully made. So therefore, I moved on.

FORGIVENESS

My hell did end there physically with the abuse although much more happened after that. More that I would be willing to share when God tells me to. What I will tell you is that through all I went through I learned to love with the love of God and forgive. I'm not going to let people run over me and I'm not going to let them control me by their actions. I am over the mess I have been through and I know it was for a purpose. It took years but I can honestly say I forgave the men who hurt me, physically, mentally and emotionally. Through it all, God has revealed Himself as a Healer, Restorer, Mind Regulator, Heart fixer, Provider, my Help, my Joy, my Strength and much more. It's not a lie when I say Jesus is my entire world. Yes I still have trials and I had to rebuild and go through a humbling process but I have peace and I am blessed. No, I am not perfect and don't pretend to be. I have testimony after testimony of how the Lord Jesus has kept me and guided me.

If you are in the midst of a storm, go through it don't stand in it. Reach up and let Jesus guide you out. He will but you have to surrender all.

If you take anything with you from this book let it be that Jesus loves you and you do matter to the Master. You are somebody. He created you in His image and you are special in the eyes of the Father, He makes no mistakes and you are no mistake.

www.ingramcontent.com/pod-product-compliance
Lightning Source LLC
Chambersburg PA
CBHW071054090426
42737CB00013B/2345